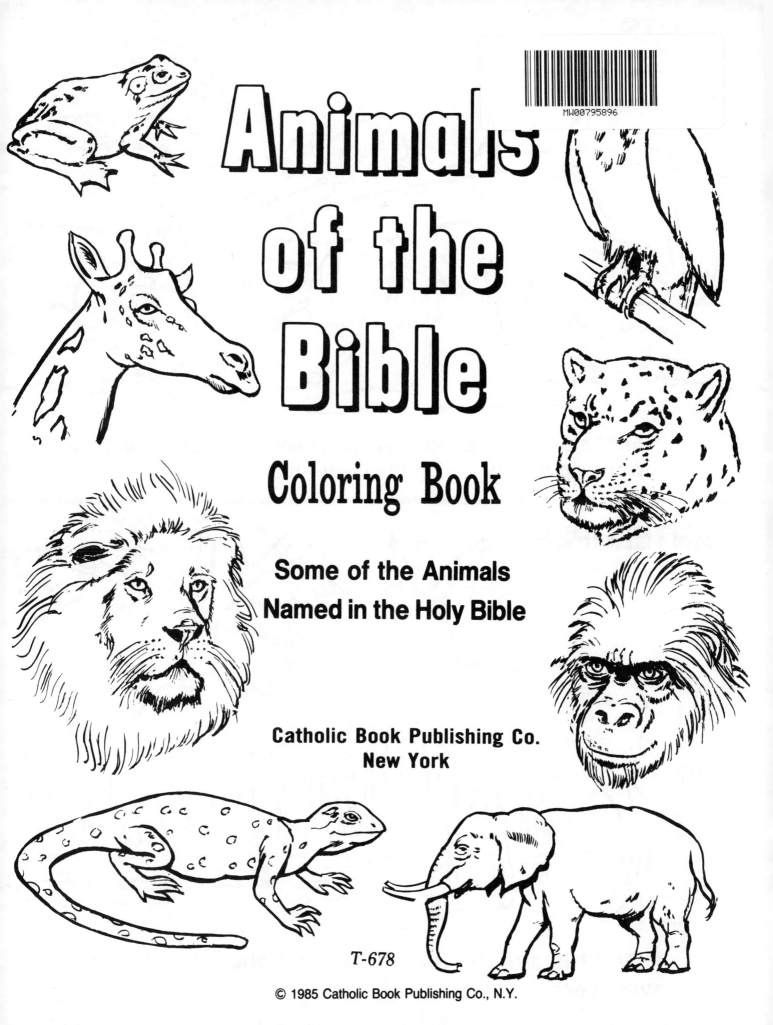

Animals of the Bible

Coloring Book

**Some of the Animals
Named in the Holy Bible**

**Catholic Book Publishing Co.
New York**

T-678

ANTS
Proverbs 30:25

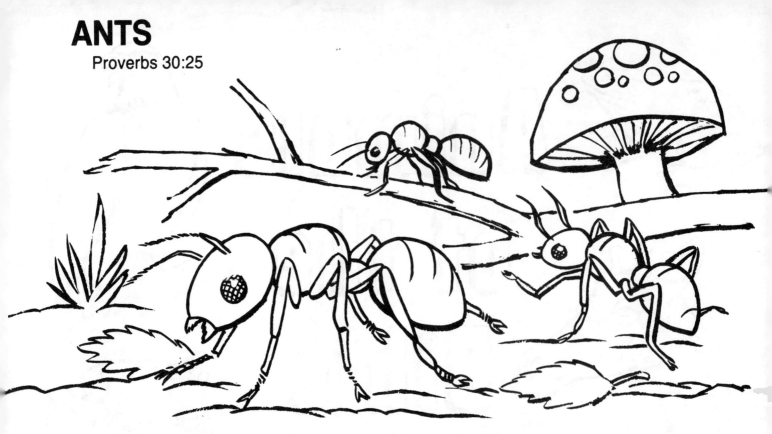

ANTS store up their food during the summer months so they won't go hungry during the winter months.

ANTELOPES
Deuteronomy 14:5

ANTELOPES are like deer, but do not shed their horns every year.

APES

2 Chronicles 9:21

APES are large animals and are considered valuable for their fur.

BATS

Leviticus 11:19

BATS are small birds and live in caves.

BEARS
1 Samuel 17:34

There are large BEARS that live in the mountains.

BEES

Psalm 81:17

BEES provided honey as food for the people.

BOAR

Psalm 80:14

BOARS are wild animals and live in wooded areas.

6

BULL
Hosea 12:12

The BULL is a symbol of strength and one of the largest animals of the land.

CALF
Leviticus 9:2

A CALF was offered as a sacrifice to God.

CAMELS
Genesis 24:61

People rode on CAMELS to travel across desert land.

CATTLE
Genesis 1:24

In the beginning, God created living creatures, including CATTLE.

COWS

1 Samuel 6:12

COWS provided milk, butter and cheese for the people.

DOGS
Job 30:1

Large DOGS protected a shepherd's flock from attack.

11

DONKEY
Matthew 21:1

Jesus rode on a DONKEY into Jerusalem.

DOVE
Genesis 8:10

After the great flood, Noah sent out a DOVE to find dry land.

EAGLE

Jeremiah 49:16

EAGLES are noted for their strength and speed as well as ability to make nests in very high places.

ELEPHANTS

1 Maccabees 1:17

ELEPHANTS were used to carry men and weapons to battle.

FISH

Genesis 1:20

God filled the waters with many different kinds of FISH.

FOXES
Judges 15:4

FOXES are noted for their speed and alertness.

FROGS
Exodus 8:1

FROGS invaded Egypt when the Pharaoh would not let the people worship the Lord.

GOATS

Luke 15:29

GOATS provided food and milk for the people.

HORSE

1 Kings 20:19

HORSES were used to pull chariots in battles and processions.

18

JACKAL

Jeremiah 9:9

JACKALS are wild animals that hunt for small animals and birds.

LAMB

Numbers 28:9

A LAMB was offered as a sacrifice to show love for the Lord.

LEOPARD
Jeremiah 13:23

LEOPARDS are strong animals with large black spots on their bodies.

LIONS

Daniel 6:23

Daniel was sent into a den of LIONS, only to be saved by God's angels.

LIZARDS

Leviticus 11:30

LIZARDS roamed the land hunting for insects and worms.

OSTRICH

Lamentations 4:3

The OSTRICH is the largest and fastest of birds with a long neck and short wings.

23

OXEN

1 Corinthians 9:9

OXEN were strong animals used for plowing the land.

PIGEONS

Leviticus 12:6

PIGEONS were offered as a sacrifice to cleanse people of their sins.

RAM

Genesis 22:9

Abraham sacrificed a RAM to show his love for the Lord.

RAVENS

1 Kings 17:4

RAVENS are large birds and the first of the wild creatures to be tamed.

26

ROOSTER

Matthew 26:31

Peter denied he knew Jesus three times before the **ROOSTER** crowed one evening.

SHEEP
Matthew 18:10

Jesus cares for every SHEEP in his flock.

SNAKE

Genesis 3:1

A **SNAKE** tempted Eve to eat the forbidden fruit in the Garden of Eden.

SPARROW

Psalm 84:4

SPARROWS are small birds and live high in the treetops.

STORK
Zechariah 5:9

The **STORK** is one of the largest birds with long legs and a long red beak.

SWALLOW

Jeremiah 8:7

Where the **SWALLOWS** fly, tells the people changes in the time of year.

WHALES

Matthew 12:40

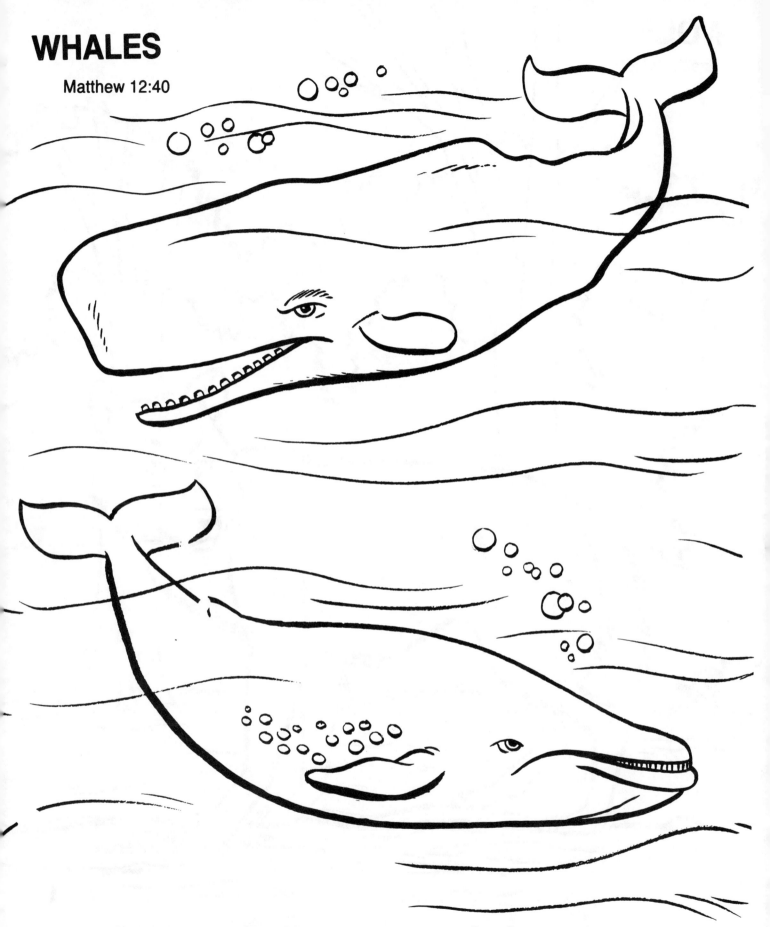

WHALES are the largest creatures in the ocean.

WOLF

Ezekiel 22:27

The WOLF was one of the cruelest animals of the land.